FACT OR FAKE?

THE TRUTH ABOUT
PLANET EARTH

SONYA NEWLAND

First published in Great Britain in 2022 by Wayland
Copyright © Hodder and Stoughton Limited, 2022

Produced for Wayland by
White-Thomson Publishing Ltd
www.wtpub.co.uk

Editor: Sonya Newland
Series Designer: Rocket Design (East Anglia) Ltd
Consultant: Steve Parker

HB ISBN: 978 1 5263 1849 7
PB ISBN: 978 1 5263 1848 0

Wayland
An imprint of
Hachette Children's Group
Part of Hodder & Stoughton
Carmelite House
50 Victoria Embankment
London EC4Y 0DZ

An Hachette UK Company
www.hachettechildrens.co.

Printed in China

Picture acknowledgements:

Shutterstock: rogistok 4, V_ctoria 5, Ameashi 6, Roman Bykhalov 7, 44–45, ankomando 8, BeRad 9, MilaArt 10–11, ArtHeart 12, ArtMari 13, 50, 83, vectorlab2D 14, ashimmah15, aksol 16, John T Takai 17, Egor Shilov 18, Ira Bagira 19, Snap2Art 20, Teguh Mujiono 21, 30, miumi 22, Good_Stock 23, Blue Flourishes 24, ChipVector 25, Pand P Studio26–27, Natali Snailcat 28, Dean Gradella 29, Moriz 31, GabrielJose 32, Kalimanorah 34, Kalimanorah 34, Rvector 35, Jemastock 36, owatta 37, Sararoom Design 38, Ohmega1982 39, newelle 40, Larry-Rains 41, VikiVector 42, Crystal_Snow 43, TAW4 46, johavel 47, Padma Sanjaya 48, vldkont 49, Valerii_M 51, wectors 52, Viktoriia_P 53, dimair 54, anastasiia ivanova 55, Aksenova Nadezhda 56, zizi_mentos 58, Anna Marin N 59, Aluna1 60–61, Croisy 62l, Incomible 62r, Marina Akinina 64, DeShoff 65, Enimados 66, Emre Tarimcioglu 67, Polina Tomtosova 68, emrcartoons.com 69, nikiteev_konstantin 70l, 84, NikomMaelao Production 70r, AmySachar 71, VectorPot 72, owatta 73, julio chaniago 7 74–75, Anna Bochkova 74–75, linoleum 77, Pyty 78, Oliver Hoffmann 79, Egor Shilov 81, kareemov1000 82, i-muistudio 85, dedMazay 89, AVA Bitter 89.

All design elements from Shutterstock or drawn by designer.

Every effort has been made to clear copyright. Should there be any inadvertent omission, please apply to the publisher for rectification.

The website addresses (URLs) included in this book were valid at the time of going to press. However, it is possible that contents or addresses may have changed since the publication of this book. No responsibility for any such changes can be accepted by either the author or the publisher.

All facts and statistics were correct at the time of press.

WEST NORTHAMPTONSHIRE COUNCIL	
60000521320	
Askews & Holts	
DD	

CAN YOU SEPARATE THE FACTS FROM THE FAKES?

OUR PLANET IS RADIOACTIVE!

WHAT?!

THE NORTH POLE IS MOVING.

NO WAY!

ANTARCTICA IS THE COLDEST PLACE ON EARTH.

(SOUNDS TRUE ...)

A DAY IS 24 HOURS LONG.

DUH!

(OR IS IT?)

Read on to find out the reality behind popular myths and mind-blowing truths about planet Earth. Discover the science behind it all and then dazzle your friends and family with amazing, bizarre — and sometimes downright unbelievable — facts about Earth.

THE NAME EARTH MEANS 'THE GROUND'

THE SCIENCE

The ancient Greeks and Romans named the planets they knew of after their gods. That's why we have Jupiter, ruler of the gods, Mars, god of war, and Venus, goddess of love. Even the planets that were discovered later were named in the same way. All except poor Earth.

FACT OR FAKE?

It's an unfortunate fact that the most interesting planet – the one we live on – has the most boring name. 'Earth' comes from words in Old English and German, 'eor(th)e' or 'erthe' and 'erde', all of which simply mean 'ground'.

I want to be named after a god!

VERDICT

Fact

EVEREST IS THE TALLEST MOUNTAIN ON EARTH

Everyone knows that Everest is the world's tallest mountain, right? Wrong! While this mighty mountain has the highest altitude, the *tallest* mountain is actually Mauna Kea, on Hawaii.

THE SCIENCE

Everest reaches higher above sea level than any other mountain – 8,848.86 m to be precise. Mauna Kea rises only 4,205 m above sea level, but it starts at the bottom of the Pacific Ocean. From its base to its summit, Mauna Kea is 9,966 m tall.

SLEEPING GIANT

Mauna Kea is actually a volcano, although it's a dormant one. It last erupted 4,600 years ago.

VERDICT
Fake

5

EARTH IS 4.5 BILLION YEARS OLD

FACT OR FAKE?

Scientists can work out how old Earth is by studying its rocks! They can find the age of rocks and minerals using a technique called radiometric (or radioactive) dating. This suggests that Earth is about 4.5 billion years old – give or take 50 million years!

THE SCIENCE

The oldest substances that occur naturally on Earth are minerals found in Australia, which are more than 4.3 billion years old. However, meteorites that have crashed to Earth have been dated to 4.5 billion years ago. As most bodies in the solar system were probably formed at the same time, scientists think this is probably Earth's age too.

Yippee! That makes me feel positively young!

VERDICT

Fact

THE SEA IS BLUE BECAUSE IT REFLECTS THE SKY

It seems clear that water is, well, clear. So why does a big expanse of water like the ocean look blue? Is it simply that it's reflecting the big blue sky? Well, it is – but only in a small way. It's really about how water absorbs light.

THE SCIENCE

White light from the Sun is actually made up of different colours. Water absorbs colours with longer wavelengths such as red, orange and yellow, leaving behind more of the shorter-wavelength blues and greens. That's what we see in the sea.

VERDICT
Fake

BLUE SKY

The sky is sometimes blue because the atmosphere scatters the blue part of sunlight more than other colours. And the sea does reflect the blue sky a tiny bit.

7

LIGHTNING
NEVER STRIKES THE
SAME PLACE
TWICE

ZAP!

THE SCIENCE

Lightning is basically a huge spark of electricity. Particles in thunderclouds collide to create an electric charge. This connects with an electric charge on the ground and causes a lightning flash. The charge on the ground often builds around tall objects, such as isolated buildings and trees, so lightning may strike these places frequently.

FACT OR FAKE?

Lightning is random. It can strike anywhere at any time, so it might seem unlikely that it would hit the same place twice. But this old adage is a total myth. Lightning often strikes the same place – and more than just twice!

VERDICT
Fake

LIGHTNING CENTRAL
The Empire State Building in New York, USA, is hit by lightning about 25 times a year.

EARTH'S SURFACE MOVES FASTER AT THE EQUATOR THAN IT DOES AT THE POLES

FACT OR FAKE?

You'd think that a planet would spin at the same speed all over, wouldn't you? In fact there's a dramatic difference! At the equator, the surface spins at nearly 1,600 kph. At the poles, it saunters round at about 0.00008 kph.

THE SCIENCE

The whole Earth makes one rotation in just less than 24 hours. But Earth is wider at the equator than it is at the poles, which means that the broad equatorial regions have to move faster to keep up.

VERDICT
Fact

PENGUINS ONLY LIVE AT THE SOUTH POLE

FACT OR FAKE?

Penguins can only be found in the southern hemisphere, but it's not true that they only live at the South Pole. There are 18 species of penguin and just two of them live only in Antarctica: emperor penguins and Adélie penguins. Penguins can be found on every continent in the southern hemisphere!

Are you from the north or the south?

VERDICT
Fake

THE SCIENCE

It's also a myth that penguins only live in cold areas. They thrive in other habitats, including deserts in South America and on the tropical Galápagos Islands. Penguins can't fly, so they prefer island life as there usually aren't as many predators.

Do I look like a puffin?

ARCTIC PENGUINS?

If you were wandering around Arctic regions, you might spot a cute black and white bird with an orange beak, a bit like a penguin. But these are puffins – sea birds that make their home in chilly northern regions.

11

THE NILE IS THE LONGEST RIVER IN THE WORLD

FACT OR FAKE?

It's not as easy as you might think to work out how long a river is. Rivers twist and turn and can be hundreds of kilometres long. And they have a habit of flowing into each other, so who's to say where one river ends and another starts? But experts generally agree that the Nile is the longest river in the world.

THE SCIENCE

The source of the Nile is Lake Victoria in eastern Africa, which is so huge it's in three countries: Tanzania, Uganda and Kenya. From there, the Nile flows 6,695 km through 11 countries.

SECOND PLACE

The Amazon River in South America comes a close second, at around 6,400 km.

VERDICT
Fact

RAIN
FALLS IN DROPS

FACT OR FAKE?

You know what a drop looks like – a kind of pear or tear shape. That's how we imagine rain as it falls from the sky. But if you could look close enough, you'd see that raindrops aren't drop-shaped. They look more like jellybeans.

THE SCIENCE

High up in Earth's atmosphere, raindrops are little spheres or balls. As they fall, they change shape. Air pushing up on the water drop flattens the bottom of it and curves it slightly, making it bean-shaped.

VERDICT

Fake

13

THERE'S A COUNTRY YOU COULD WALK ALL THE WAY ROUND IN AN HOUR

FACT OR FAKE?

Not all countries are huge, and you don't always need a plane or even a car to travel around one. In fact, you could stroll from one side of the smallest country in the world to the other in about 15 minutes!

THE SCIENCE

Vatican City lies completely within Italy's capital, Rome. But it's an independent country, with its own flag, anthem and even stamps! This tiny state covers just half a square kilometre and is home to about 800 people – including the Pope.

VERDICT
Fact

A DAY ON EARTH IS 24 HOURS LONG

FACT OR FAKE?

Sixty seconds in a minute ...
60 minutes in an hour ...
24 hours in a day ... that's how
we measure time. Except that
if you want to be *really* precise
about it, a day isn't actually
24 hours long – it's 23 hours,
56 minutes and 4.096 seconds.

THE SCIENCE

That's the time it takes Earth
to spin once on its axis (the
sidereal day). But as Earth
moves round the Sun, it needs
to turn just a tiny bit further
every day for the Sun to be in
the same position in the sky
as seen from Earth (the solar
day). That distance accounts
for the missing four minutes.

HOW LONG IS A YEAR?

Think a year is 365 days long?
Think again! A year lasts 365 days,
5 hours, 48 minutes and 46 seconds
(apart from leap years).

VERDICT **Fake**

GLACIERS FLOW LIKE RIVERS

People tend to think of glaciers as like large lakes of ice, fixed in one spot. But glaciers are actually moving – although they flow very slowly compared to the speeds that rivers can reach!

THE SCIENCE

It's the sheer weight of all that ice that causes glaciers to move. As they flow slowly downhill, they shape the landscape around them. Glaciers are so powerful they can even carve a path through mountain rocks.

FAST FLOW?
Most glaciers flow at a rate of about 25 cm per day, but the fastest glacier, the Jakobshavn Isbrae in Greenland, speeds along at about 40 m a day!

VERDICT
Fact

EARTH WAS ONCE ONE SINGLE SUPERCONTINENT

FACT OR FAKE?

Today there are several continents – all of them familiar shapes on a globe. But this isn't how Earth always looked. Around 280 million years ago, there was just one giant landmass, called Pangaea. That meant there was one giant ocean too, known as Panthalassa.

THE SCIENCE

Pangaea formed about 335 million years ago. It was there when the dinosaurs appeared around 235 million years ago. From about 175 million years ago, the supercontinent slowly broke apart. The pieces drifted into the positions we know today. But beware – they're still moving!

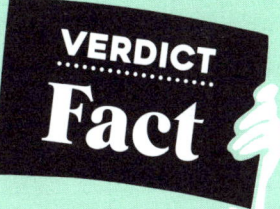

VERDICT
Fact

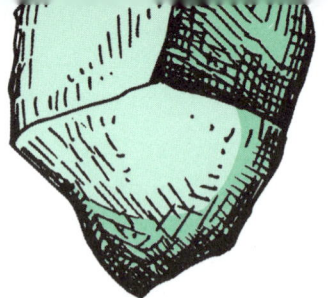

ROCKS ARE
HEAVY

If you dropped a rock on your foot from a big enough height it would probably hurt a bit. And you can certainly find some super-heavy rocks on Earth. But other rocks are so light that they can float on water.

Pumice is a type of volcanic rock. It forms when magma from a volcano cools quickly in water. Pumice looks a bit like a grey sponge, with lots of air bubbles. These give the rock a lower density than water, which means it can float.

ROCK RAFT

In 2019, trillions of pieces of pumice were found floating in the Pacific Ocean. This 'rock raft' was the size of 20,000 football pitches!

VERDICT
Fake

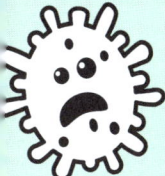

THERE ARE MORE THAN A BILLION MICROBES IN A TEASPOON OF SOIL

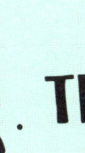

THE SCIENCE

Microbes are everywhere on planet Earth. They're in the air you breathe and the water you drink. They're all over your skin, and even inside your body. Luckily, they're so small you can't see them. In fact, they're so minuscule that about a billion of them can fit into a single teaspoon of soil.

Scientists measure teeny tiny organisms in units called micrometres. One micrometre is one thousandth of a millimetre. Most microbes are around 1 micrometre – so imagine how many of them could be living up your nose right now!

VERDICT

Fact

YOU CAN ONLY SEE AN AURORA NEAR THE NORTH POLE

FACT OR FAKE?

The aurora borealis, also known as the Northern Lights, only happens over or near the North Pole. But this isn't the only aurora! The same amazing light display happens at the South Pole, where it's known as the aurora australis (the Southern Lights).

THE SCIENCE

The dancing lights of an aurora are caused by the solar wind, which sends out tiny particles called electrons. Following Earth's magnetic field, the electrons bash into atoms of gases in the high atmosphere, making the atoms glow different colours.

SPACE GLOW

The aurora happens 200–300 km above Earth, and is bright enough to be seen from space too.

VERDICT
Fake

HURRICANES ONLY HAPPEN IN THE TROPICS

FACT OR FAKE?

The tropics are the areas near the equator. The Sun is very strong in the tropics, so they're the warmest places on Earth. And hurricanes eat heat! These huge, dangerous weather systems only form in tropical areas. In fact, another name for a hurricane is a tropical cyclone.

THE SCIENCE

Hurricanes form over tropical seas. They move along, sucking up warm air and picking up strength as they go. As the air rises, it cools to form clouds and thunderstorms in an enormous swirling mass. Global warming is causing sea temperatures to rise, resulting in more hurricanes.

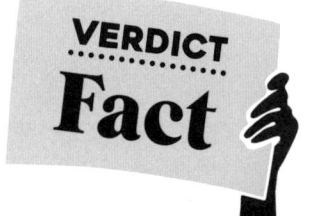

VERDICT
Fact

21

THERE ARE MORE THAN 60,000 SPECIES OF TREE

22

FACT OR FAKE?

If you want to be really accurate, there are 60,065 tree species on Earth. Or so the experts say. There may be more, of course, hiding in parts of the planet where people rarely go, but these are the ones we know about.

THE SCIENCE

Brazil can claim the most species of any country. Thanks to its rainforests, 8,715 tree species can be found there! Of all tree species, more than half can only be found in one country.

VERDICT

Fact

HAILSTONES ARE FROZEN RAINDROPS

BONK!

FACT OR FAKE?

Rain, snow, sleet, hail ... these are types of precipitation (that's water in the atmosphere to you and me). But they aren't all simply different versions of the same thing. Each type of precipitation forms in a different way.

THE SCIENCE

Hailstones are formed when drops of water freeze together high up in cold storm clouds. The chunks of ice eventually get so heavy that they drop to Earth. Frozen rain is different. It falls in liquid form and only freezes as it nears the ground.

A SHOWER OF ... GRAUPELS?

A 'hailstone' that is soft, white and measures less than 5 mm across isn't actually a hailstone – it's a graupel!

VERDICT

Fake

23

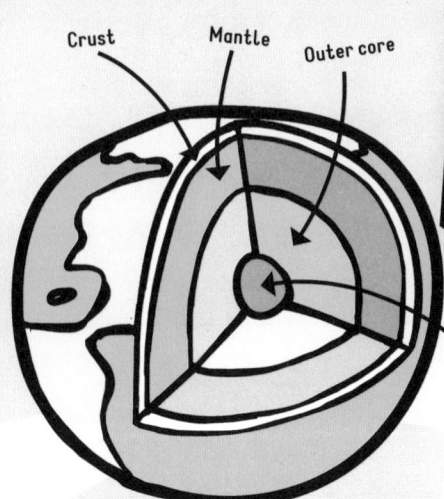

Crust
Mantle
Outer core
Inner core

EARTH HAS FOUR LAYERS

FACT OR FAKE?

Earth seems like a pretty solid structure, but you're actually standing (or sitting, or maybe even lying) on one – relatively thin – part of it. Our onion-like planet is actually made up of four layers: crust, mantle, outer core and inner core.

THE SCIENCE

Let's work from the inside out. The hot inner core is solid metal, while the outer core is boiling liquid metal. The mantle is the largest layer, 2,900 km thick and made of melted iron and semi-solid rocks that can move about. In contrast, the solid rocky crust is really thin, only about 35–70 km deep.

THE MOVING MANTLE

Earthquakes and volcanic eruptions are caused by rocks in the mantle crashing into each other.

VERDICT
Fact

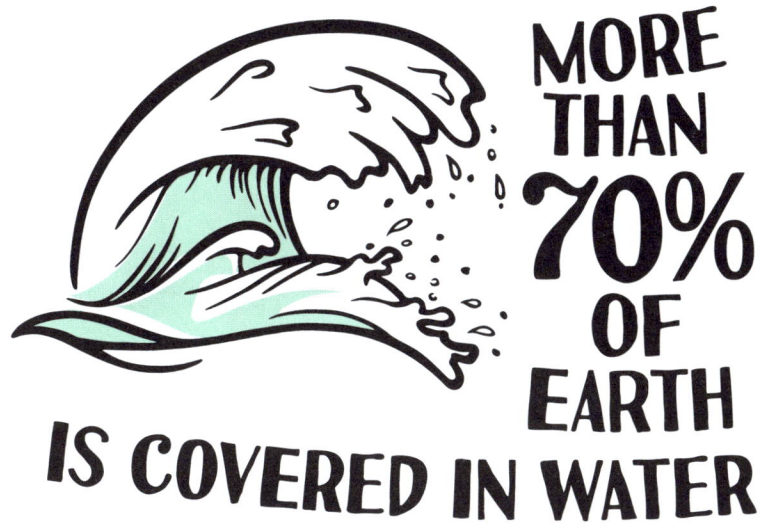

MORE THAN 70% OF EARTH IS COVERED IN WATER

FACT OR FAKE?

They don't call Earth the 'blue planet' for nothing. Images of Earth from space show it looking like a blue marble, swirled with brown and green land and topped with white clouds. It looks this way because about 71 per cent of Earth's surface is water.

THE SCIENCE

Most of this is the oceans – 96.5 per cent of all water on Earth, in fact. The rest is in rivers and lakes, but also in frozen water such as glaciers and ice caps. It also exists as water vapour in the air. All this water is constantly moving around in a process called the water cycle.

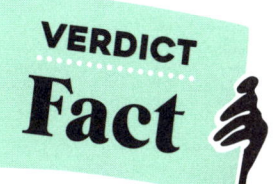

VERDICT

Fact

CLIMATE CHANGE HAS BEEN HAPPENING FOREVER

FACT OR FAKE?

Our planet is 4.5 billion years old. During that time the climate has changed a lot. In fact, it's gone through several periods of warming and cooling, so it's true that changes like this are part of a natural process. But that's not what we mean when we talk about climate change today.

IT'S ALL ABOUT THE GAS

Human-made climate change is caused by gas. The world started heating up much quicker when we began pumping carbon dioxide into the air from factories and cars.

THE SCIENCE

Things are happening much faster than they should. Climate changes that once took place really slowly (over hundreds of thousands of years) are now happening in just a few years. The world is warmer now than it's ever been – at least since records began.

VERDICT

Fake

THE GREAT BARRIER REEF IS THE LARGEST LIVING STRUCTURE

FACT OR FAKE?

Stretching for 2,300 km off the coast of north-eastern Australia, the Great Barrier Reef covers an area bigger than Germany! It's the largest coral reef in the world. And because corals are living things, it's also the largest living organism on the planet.

THE SCIENCE

The Great Barrier Reef is actually around 3,000 separate reefs. Corals, which the reefs are made of, look like tiny plants, but are actually sea creatures. The reefs they build are home to more than a thousand species of fish.

VERDICT
Fact

VIEW FROM SPACE

Astronauts reported that they could see the Great Barrier Reef from the Moon!

THE MOON IS EARTH'S ONLY NATURAL SATELLITE

I thought I was special!

FACT OR FAKE?

A satellite is any object that moves around another object in space, and moons are natural satellites of the planets they orbit. Look into the night sky and you'll see just one Moon near Earth. But is it really alone? Astronomers are now pretty sure it isn't!

THE SCIENCE

In 1961, Polish astronomer Kazimierz Kordylewski glimpsed what he thought were two ghostly 'dust moons' orbiting Earth. No one was sure exactly what they were, but in 2018 it was confirmed that these orbiting clouds really exist. They're about 400,000 km away – roughly the same distance as the Moon.

VERDICT
Fake

FOSSILS ARE THE REMAINS OF ANCIENT LIVING THINGS

FACT OR FAKE?

Can you tell the difference between a fossil and an ordinary rock? While rocks are just clumps of minerals, fossils are the remains of creatures that were once alive, which have turned to stone over millions of years.

THE SCIENCE

After a living thing dies, the soft parts of the body, such as flesh and muscle, decay. The hard parts, like bones, are buried by tiny pieces of rock called sediment. This builds up in layers over many years. Eventually the bones are dissolved and replaced by minerals from water, which create a replica of the bone within the rock.

FIGHTING FOSSILS

Fossils of the dinosaurs *Velociraptor* and *Protoceratops* have been found preserved mid-fight! The *Protoceratops* was biting the *Velociraptor*'s arm.

VERDICT
Fact

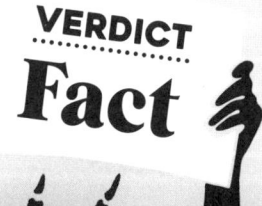

ANIMALS CAN PREDICT EARTHQUAKES

Run for your lives!

FACT OR FAKE?

Since ancient times, people have believed that animals have a kind of sixth sense, which alerts them to danger. There are stories of animals suddenly taking to their heels, bees inexplicably abandoning their hives, dogs howling inconsolably – all just before earthquakes occur.

THE SCIENCE

Not even earthquake experts know when a quake is going to strike, so animals can't *predict* them. But it's possible that, with their heightened senses, they can detect changes in the air or vibrations in the earth before humans can. This may be what gives them a head start when fleeing from natural disasters.

VERDICT

Fake

31

THE NORTH POLE IS MOVING

NORTH POLE

In the year 1900, Earth's magnetic North Pole was in Canada. In the year 2000, it was nearer Greenland. Now it's heading towards Siberia at a speed of 40–50 km per year. It's definitely on the move!

THE SCIENCE

The magnetic poles move because of what's going on at Earth's core. There, liquid iron surges and swirls, pulling on Earth's magnetic field and changing the position of the poles. These changes have been happening faster in recent years – and scientists don't know why exactly.

VERDICT

Fact

THE LITHOSPHERE IS PART OF EARTH'S ATMOSPHERE

Troposphere, stratosphere, mesosphere, thermosphere ... our planet's atmosphere has several layers, but the lithosphere isn't one of them. That's actually what you're standing on: the solid outer layer of Earth's crust.

THE SCIENCE

Here on Earth we're surrounded by 'spheres'. Some are part of the atmosphere ('air sphere'). There's also the hydrosphere ('water sphere') – all the rivers, lakes, seas and oceans – and the exosphere ('outside sphere'), which stretches about 200,000 km beyond our planet. Lithosphere means 'rock sphere'.

LIFE SPHERE

The biosphere, or 'life sphere', is the word for all living things, including plants, trees, birds, animals, bacteria – and you – plus the places they live.

VERDICT
....
Fake

33

GRAVITY IS THE SAME WHEREVER YOU ARE ON EARTH

FACT OR FAKE?

If you went to the Moon, you'd quickly notice a difference in the strength of gravity. Here on Earth, it seems like gravity is the same wherever you go, but in fact at ground level gravity is very slightly stronger than it is at the top of a mountain , for example.

THE SCIENCE

Gravity is the invisible force of attraction between objects, and its strength depends on the size of the objects and how close they are to each other. Bigger, closer objects have a greater gravitational pull. At the top of a mountain, you're farther from the planet's centre of gravity than you are lower down, so the gravity between you and Earth is less.

VERDICT
Fake

THE EQUATOR MARKS 0° LATITUDE

FACT OR FAKE?

Earth is covered in imaginary lines and points: the poles, the equator, a whole grid of lines of longitude and latitude. All these help us know where we are on our home planet. Latitude is the distance north or south of the equator, so the equator itself lies at 0°.

THE SCIENCE

Lines of latitude are called parallels. Each parallel measures one degree, which represents 60 minutes. Everywhere on Earth has a latitude measured in degrees and minutes. For example, London is 51° 30′ N, which means it is 51 degrees and 30 minutes north of the equator.

POLAR POINTS

The latitude of the North Pole is 90° N and the South Pole is (logically therefore) 90° S.

VERDICT

Fact

35

IT'S WARM IN SUMMER BECAUSE EARTH IS CLOSER TO THE SUN

It's true that in the southern hemisphere, Earth is closer to the Sun in summer than winter. But in the northern hemisphere, the opposite is true – Earth is further from the Sun in summer. And yet it's still warmer at that time of year.

THE SCIENCE

The seasons happen because Earth is slightly tilted on its axis. This means that in summer the Sun's rays hit Earth at a steep angle. The Sun's heat and light are concentrated on a smaller area, which increases the temperature. In winter, rays hit Earth at a shallower angle, spreading over a larger area so there's less heat to go around.

VERDICT
Fake

ANTARCTICA IS THE COLDEST PLACE ON EARTH

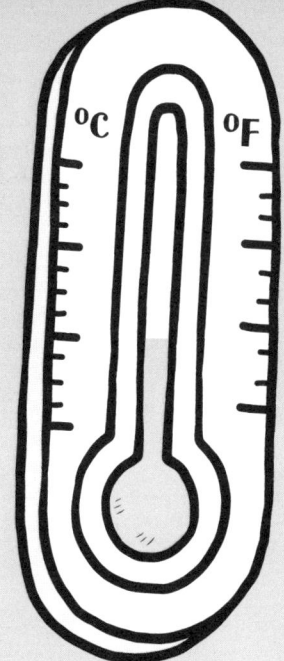

FACT OR FAKE?

It's *unbelievably* cold in Antarctica. In fact, four of the five lowest temperatures ever recorded on Earth are on this freezing continent. Record-holders include satellite measurements on the East Antarctic Plateau which go as low as –98° C!

THE SCIENCE

Both the Arctic and the Antarctic are cold because they don't get any direct sunlight. Even at the height of summer, the Sun sits low in the sky. The Antarctic is colder because the circulating water under the Arctic ice is warmer than the deep-frozen ground of Antarctica.

AT THE OTHER EXTREME ...

The hottest place on the planet is generally accepted to be Furnace Creek, in Death Valley, California. Average summer temperatures there reach 47° C!

VERDICT
Fact

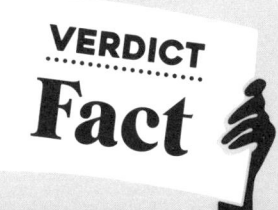

EARTH'S CORE IS AS HOT AS THE SUN

It's hard to know exactly how hot things get right in the middle of Earth. After all, scientists can hardly pop down there and take its temperature. But using some clever calculations, experts think that it's a sweltering 6,000° C at Earth's core – about the same temperature as the surface of the Sun.

THE SCIENCE

Earth's core has two layers. The outer core is so hot that the metals it's made of, iron and nickel, are liquid. But it's the inner core that's the hottest part. Despite the intense heat, the heart of our planet is solid metal because it's under so much pressure from all the outer layers (see page 24).

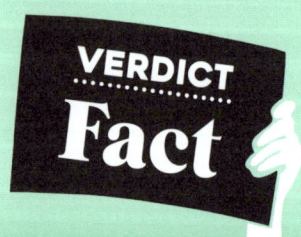

VERDICT
Fact

38

THERE ARE SEVEN CONTINENTS

FACT OR FAKE?

What *is* a continent exactly? Well, we all agree that it's one of Earth's huge landmasses – dry land surrounded (or nearly) by water. What people can't quite agree on is how many of them there are. Most say there are seven, but others argue there are only six.

THE SCIENCE

The usual seven are Africa, Antarctica, Asia, Australia, Europe, North America and South America. But in some parts of the world, North and South America are combined as a single continent. And sometimes Antarctica is also dropped from the list.

HIDDEN LAND

Scientists may have found a whole new continent – a landmass submerged in the ocean beneath New Zealand. They call it Zealandia.

VERDICT
....
Fake
(OR MAYBE FACT!)

RIVERS FLOW FROM NORTH TO SOUTH

FACT OR FAKE?

Is south always down and north always up? Gravity means that rivers will flow downhill, but that doesn't mean they have to move in a southerly direction! Rivers can – and do – flow northwards. And eastwards and westwards too, for that matter.

THE SCIENCE

Rivers tend to follow the path with the fewest obstacles from their origin (the headwater) to their destination (the mouth). This usually means that they'll end up winding in several different directions along their course.

THE NORTHWARDS NILE

The Nile starts in south-east Africa and flows northwards for more than 6,600 km to the Mediterranean Sea.

VERDICT

Fake

THERE ARE NO SHARKS IN ANTARCTICA

Brrrrr ...

FACT OR FAKE?

Sharks can be found in almost all ocean habitats, from coral reefs in warm tropical seas to the chilly waters under the Arctic ice in the far north. But there's one place you could swim without fear of sharks – and that's Antarctica.

THE SCIENCE

The oceans around the southern continent are simply too cold for sharks – and many other marine creatures too. It wasn't always that way, though. Until 40 million years ago, the waters were warm enough for sharks to happily inhabit them. As global temperatures rise, sharks might once again swim around the South Pole.

VERDICT
Fact

41

LAKE SUPERIOR
LAKE EVEN MORE SUPERIOR

LAKE SUPERIOR IS THE LARGEST LAKE IN THE WORLD

FACT OR FAKE?

Lake Superior is one of the five Great Lakes, which straddle the border between the USA and Canada. Its name certainly suggests that it's superior to all other lakes. But it's actually a misleadingly named body of water that holds the title of largest lake – the Caspian Sea.

THE SCIENCE

A lake is defined as a large area of water that's completely surrounded by land, so the landlocked Caspian Sea counts as a lake – albeit a salty one! It borders five countries: Kazakhstan, Russia, Turkmenistan, Azerbaijan and Iran.

COUNTRY COMPARISONS

The Caspian Sea has an area nearly the same size as Japan, the 62nd largest country in the world. By contrast, Lake Superior is less than one-quarter the area of the Caspian Sea.

VERDICT
Fake

42

EARTH IS A PERFECT SPHERE

Don't want to get out of shape!

FACT OR FAKE?

The pictures you've seen of Earth from space make it look like a perfect round marble, don't they? But what you can't see clearly in those pictures is that the North and South Poles are slightly flatter.

THE SCIENCE

All spinning objects experience force. The faster the spin, the greater the force. The effect of this force on the fast-spinning Earth is to 'stretch' it slightly at the equator so it bulges out. This causes a flattening at the poles.

VERDICT

Fake

AROUND 75% OF THE WORLD'S VOLCANOES ARE IN ONE REGION

FACT OR FAKE?

It's true. Around three-quarters of all the volcanoes on Earth (more than 450 of them) can be found in a single zone, known as the Pacific Ring of Fire. Some of the volcanoes here are dormant, but many of them are active, and eruptions are common.

THE SCIENCE

The ring is actually an arc, straddling the equator and stretching roughly 40,000 km through the Pacific Ocean. Here, the massive tectonic plates below the surface of Earth move around a lot. As these plates grind past each other, fiery magma is created. And where there's magma, there are usually volcanoes!

EARTHQUAKE EPICENTRE

Around 90 per cent of all earthquakes that happen on Earth take place within the Pacific Ring of Fire.

VERDICT

Fact

AROUND 80% OF THE OCEAN IS UNEXPLORED

FACT OR FAKE?

Sometimes it feels like there can't be a single corner of the world that humans haven't explored. While there are indeed only a few remote and inaccessible places left for us to poke our noses into on Earth's surface, it's a whole different story under water.

THE SCIENCE

More than 80 per cent of Earth's oceans remain a mystery to us. They're simply too deep and too dark for humans to explore properly. Even using modern equipment such as underwater vehicles and sonar for mapping the sea floor, we only know a fraction of what goes on down there. There could be millions of unknown species lurking in the depths!

VERDICT

Fact

EARTH HAS THE FEWEST MOONS OF ALL THE PLANETS

FACT OR FAKE?

One rocky moon doesn't seem a lot – not when you consider that Jupiter has about 79 moons and Saturn has more than 80! But not all the planets are lucky enough to have even one companion. Poor old Mercury and Venus don't have any moons at all.

THE SCIENCE

Mercury and Venus are the two planets closest to the Sun, which probably explains their lack of moons. Too far from the planet and a moon would be sucked into the Sun. Too near and it would be destroyed by gravity. Earth is just far enough away for the Moon to have formed and orbit happily.

MARS'S MOONS
Move one planet further out from the Sun and you meet Mars, which has two moons.

VERDICT
....
Fake

47

CLOUDS CAN PREDICT THE WEATHER

THE SCIENCE

You don't need special sensing equipment – or even an app on your phone – to know what's going to happen with the weather. Wherever you are, just look up! The clouds will tell you everything you need to know.

Different types of clouds form depending on what's going on in the atmosphere. Wispy cirrus clouds might suggest that rain will arrive in about 8–20 hours. Streaks of grey pannus clouds mean take your umbrella because rain is imminent. Fluffy cumulus clouds in a blue sky mean it won't rain for the rest of the day.

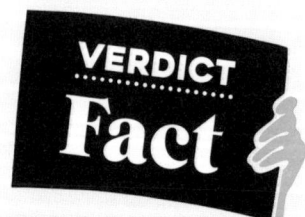

VERDICT
Fact

48

IF GLOBAL WARMING WAS REAL,

IT WOULDN'T BE COLD

FACT OR FAKE?

Global warming is a big problem on planet Earth. And it's not helped by people who argue that it's not really happening because they still have to wear a woolly hat in winter! The science is much more complicated than that ...

THE SCIENCE

Our world is getting warmer – that's just a fact. But that doesn't mean the end of cold weather right away. Global warming causes more *extreme* weather conditions, including intense storms, droughts and heatwaves.

WEATHER AND CLIMATE

Weather is what's going on outside right now – wind, rain, snow, etc. Climate is patterns of weather over a long period of time. Global warming is one of the causes of climate change (see page 26).

VERDICT

Fake

49

EARTH'S TECTONIC PLATES ARE THE SAME SHAPE AS THE CONTINENTS

FACT OR FAKE?

Deep in the ground beneath your feet, in the lithosphere (see page 33), Earth's surface is broken up into huge pieces, called tectonic plates. But these are not the same as the landmasses we know as continents, which are part of Earth's crust.

THE SCIENCE

Earth's curved surface is fractured like a jigsaw into seven major plates and more than 10 smaller ones, which lie beneath both land and sea. Tectonic plates are constantly on the move, grinding past, over and under each other at their boundaries.

VERDICT
....
Fake

HALF THE WORLD'S FORESTS ARE IN JUST FIVE COUNTRIES

FACT OR FAKE?

Around 30 per cent of land on our planet is covered in forest. And amazingly, more than half of all the forests on Earth can be found in only five countries: Russia, Brazil, Canada, the USA and China. This can be a problem because it means that just a few nations control this important resource.

THE SCIENCE

Forests are an essential ecosystem on Earth. They absorb carbon dioxide and create oxygen for us to breathe. They provide humans with food and materials such as wood. They are also home to thousands of species of plants and animals.

DANGEROUS DEFORESTATION

It's estimated that an area of forest the size of the UK is lost every year to deforestation.

VERDICT
Fact

GREENLAND IS THE
LARGEST ISLAND ON EARTH

FACT OR FAKE?

An island is any area of land that is surrounded by water, unconnected to any other land. By this definition, Greenland is more than just the largest island – it's the largest by a very long way. In fact, it's more than twice the size of the second-largest island, New Guinea.

THE SCIENCE

If Greenland was a country (it's actually part of Denmark), counting both the land and sea area it would be the 12th largest in the world. This frozen island, lying between the Arctic and North Atlantic oceans, has a population of only about 56,000.

ISLAND CONTINENT
Strictly speaking, Australia is an island, but it's also a continent so it doesn't count!

VERDICT
Fact

SOLAR POWER ONLY WORKS WHEN IT'S SUNNY

FACT OR FAKE?

The whole point of renewable resources like the Sun, wind and water is that they'll never run out. That's what makes them so great! But if you think about it, the Sun isn't *always* beaming down bright rays for solar panels to turn into electricity. So what happens when it's cloudy?

THE SCIENCE

The Sun doesn't simply stop working on overcast days. It's still there, behind the clouds, lighting up our world. It's true that panels don't gather quite as much sunlight on wintry days, but they're still pretty effective.

VERDICT
....
Fake

Here's puny Mount Everest upside down!

THE DEEPEST PLACE ON EARTH IS DEEPER THAN MOUNT EVEREST IS HIGH

FACT OR FAKE?

Far, far down in the darkest depths of the Pacific Ocean lies the deepest place on Earth. The Mariana Trench is 11,034 m deep – so deep that if you put Mount Everest at the bottom of the trench, its peak would still be 2,133 m from the top!

THE SCIENCE

The Mariana Trench is a vast crack in the ocean floor, formed around 180 million years ago by movement of Earth's tectonic plates. It's more than 2,500 km long and nearly 70 km wide.

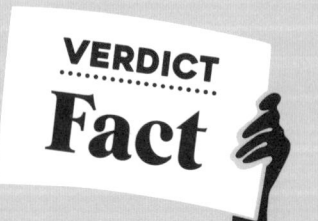

VERDICT
Fact

THE UNDERWORLD

Ocean trenches make up an area of planet Earth called the hadal zone, named after Hades, the Greek god of the underworld.

EARTH IS THE ONLY PLANET THAT HAS SOLAR ECLIPSES

FACT OR FAKE?

A solar eclipse is that eerie event when day turns to night as the Moon blocks light from the Sun. Here on Earth, eclipses happen up to four times a year. But is this an occurrence unique to our home planet?

THE SCIENCE

For an eclipse to take place, a planet, its moon and the Sun have to be completely lined up. The moon also has to be big enough to be seen to cover the disk of the Sun from the planet's surface. That rules out Mercury, Venus and Mars, but the four outer planets – Jupiter, Saturn, Uranus and Neptune – can all have solar eclipses.

VERDICT
....
Fake

MOST OF OUR OXYGEN COMES FROM TREES

FACT OR FAKE?

Without oxygen, we'd all be dead as dodos. Almost no living thing can survive without this essential gas. Fortunately, trees actually make oxygen – and there are plenty of them around to keep our air supplied. But while we can thank the rainforests for about one-third of our oxygen, almost all the rest (around 70 per cent) comes from *marine* plants.

THE SCIENCE

Marine plants, such as kelp and phytoplankton, are found within the world's vast oceans. These amazing oxygen-producing organisms use photosynthesis, just like other plants. They absorb sunlight and carbon dioxide and convert it to the life-giving gas.

VERDICT

Fake

HURRICANES ROTATE CLOCKWISE

FACT OR FAKE?

It might feel like hurricane winds blow every which way, but from above, you could see it spiralling in a particular direction. That direction depends on where in the world it is. In the southern hemisphere, hurricanes rotate clockwise, but in the northern hemisphere they go anticlockwise.

THE SCIENCE

It's all because of something called the Coriolis effect. As winds blow towards the equator, their path is deflected by the Earth's spin so they 'bend'. The air is pulled to the right in the northern hemisphere and the left in the southern hemisphere.

SPEEDY SPIRAL
The whirling winds of a hurricane can reach speeds of 320 kph – powerful enough to bring down buildings!

VERDICT
Fake

57

THE NORTH POLE
IS IN THE
MIDDLE OF THE OCEAN

FACT OR FAKE?

Most of the Arctic – the northernmost part of our planet – is covered by the Arctic Ocean. And that includes the North Pole! However, the pole isn't submerged in the freezing depths because the area is mostly covered in large chunks of shifting sea ice.

THE SCIENCE

Despite the fact that it covers more than 14 million square kilometres – about one and a half times the size of the USA – the Arctic is the world's smallest ocean. It's also the one that's warming up fastest because of climate change.

ALL ADRIFT

Because this area of the Arctic moves around on a shifting ice pack, scientists studying the pole have built drifting research stations that float around too!

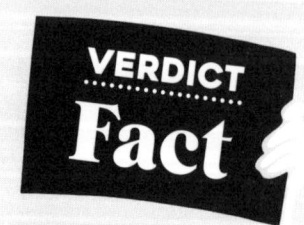

VERDICT
Fact

58

EARTH'S ATMOSPHERE IS MOSTLY OXYGEN

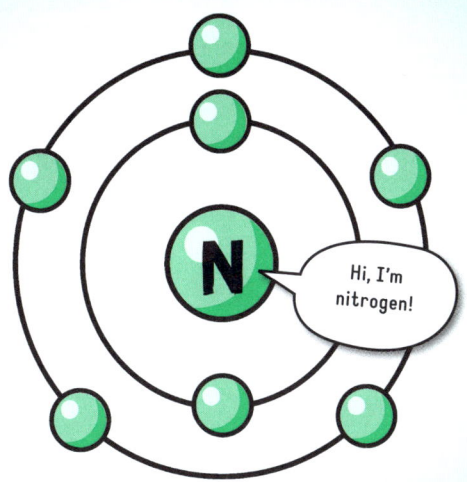

FACT OR FAKE?

Oxygen is certainly one of the most abundant chemical elements on Earth (which is good, because we'd all die without it). But it's not the most common gas in our atmosphere. That title goes to **N**itrogen.

THE SCIENCE

Nitrogen makes up a huge 78 per cent of our atmosphere. And while oxygen grabs all the gratitude for life on Earth, nitrogen is also vital for life. Plants can't grow without nitrogen, so we'd have no food source. It's also a building block of DNA – the bits inside your body that make you who you are.

VERDICT
Fake

THE SAHARA IS THE LARGEST DESERT ON EARTH

The Sahara desert covers 9.2 million square kilometres. That's nearly the size of China, and as China is the third largest country in the world, it's safe to say that the Sahara is a pretty big desert. But is it the biggest? Actually, no. It's the largest *hot* desert in the world, but here's a secret: deserts can be cold. And they don't come colder – or bigger – than the Antarctic desert.

60

THE SCIENCE

At 14.2 million square kilometres, the Antarctic desert covers almost the entire continent of Antarctica. It's basically a vast sheet of ice, averaging 1.6 km deep. Only 2 per cent of Antarctica, around the coast, isn't ice-covered. This is where all life on the continent, such as penguins and seals, lives.

DESERT DEFINITION
A desert is defined as an area that gets less than 250 mm of rain or snow a year. Some parts of the Antarctic desert get less than 100 mm!

VERDICT
Fake

THE EQUINOXES ARE THE LONGEST AND SHORTEST DAYS OF THE YEAR

FACT OR FAKE?

The clue is in the name – Earth's two equinoxes are the days of the year when day and night are of *equal* length. The word comes from the Latin, meaning 'equal night'. We get one in spring and one in autumn.

THE SCIENCE

The equinoxes happen about 20 March and 22 September. These are the two points when the Sun, on Earth's yearly journey around it, is directly over the equator.

LONG AND SHORT

The summer and winter solstices are the longest and shortest days of the year, when the Sun is furthest north or south of the equator.

VERDICT
Fake

EARTH IS MOSTLY MADE OF

IRON

FACT OR FAKE?

It seems like Earth must mostly be made of different types of rock, right? But if you could split up our planet into piles of all the different materials it's made of, the biggest pile would be metal. And most of that metal would be iron.

THE SCIENCE

Iron makes up 32.1 per cent of Earth, but most of it – 88 per cent – is right at the planet's core. In second place is oxygen (30.1 per cent), but this great gas is much more abundant at Earth's surface, of course. There, 47 per cent of the planet is oxygen!

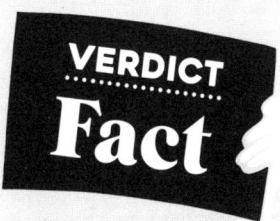

VERDICT
Fact

ROCKS ARE RECYCLED

FACT OR FAKE?

Earth is the ultimate recycling machine. Natural substances, whether they're gases, liquids or solids, are constantly changing form and being recycled and reused in 'cycles'. One of these is the rock cycle.

THE SCIENCE

Rocks are on a continuous journey. On Earth's surface, small pieces of rock settle on the bottom of rivers and seas. They are packed together and harden into solid layers. Heat deep within Earth can turn the rock to magma. Eventually it bursts back above ground as lava from volcanoes. The process takes millions of years.

THE BIG THREE

There are three main types of rock on Earth igneous, sedimentary and metamorphic. They all move round the rock cycle.

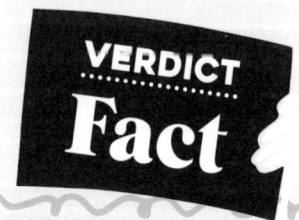

VERDICT
Fact

ANGEL FALLS IS THE WORLD'S TALLEST WATERFALL

FACT OR FAKE?

Angel Falls, in Venezuela, is often named as the tallest waterfall in the world. With a crashing drop of 979 m, the falls are definitely the highest ... if you only count those above ground. But hiding in the waters of the Denmark Strait, between Iceland and Greenland, is a waterfall that leaves all the others standing.

THE SCIENCE

How can you have an underwater waterfall? Well, cold water is heavier than warm water. When very cold water from the Nordic Sea meets the warmer waters in the Strait, it sinks rapidly and flows over a massive drop in the ocean floor. The Denmark Strait cataract, as it's called, is a staggering three times the height of Angel Falls.

VERDICT
············
Fake

AT MIDDAY, THE SUN IS DIRECTLY OVERHEAD

FACT OR FAKE?

We think of noon as the point in the day when the Sun is right above us in the sky. But the fact is, the Sun is only ever *directly* overhead – straight up – twice a year. And even then that's only the case in certain parts of the world.

THE SCIENCE

Earth isn't upright – it's slightly tilted on its axis. So, as it makes its journey round the Sun each year, you have to be within a certain distance above or below the equator for the Sun to pass directly overhead. It only happens on the summer and winter solstices in the tropics.

CANCER AND CAPRICORN

The areas where this occurs are the Tropic of Cancer (23.4°north of the equator) and the Tropic of Capricorn (23.4° south).

VERDICT

Fake

THE HIMALAYAS WERE FORMED BY TECTONIC PLATES

FACT OR FAKE?

Earth's tectonic plates are the cause of all sorts of activity on the land far above them, including earthquakes and volcanic eruptions. They're also the reason why we have mountain ranges like the huge Himalayas.

THE SCIENCE

Around 40–50 million years ago, plate movement caused a big collision between what were then two separate landmasses – India and Eurasia. Instead of one plate sinking beneath the other, the huge pressure forced the boundary upwards, creating the jagged, rocky peaks of the Himalayas.

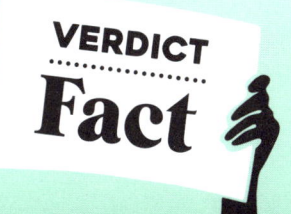

VERDICT

Fact

VOLCANOES START SMOKING BEFORE THEY ERUPT

FACT OR FAKE?

As any volcanologist will tell you, that greyish cloud you see puffing out of volcanoes isn't really smoke. The source of real smoke is burning matter, but in an active volcano, any plant matter or other stuff that could burn would have done so long ago. So what is that 'smoke'?

THE SCIENCE

It's actually a mixture of gases: water vapour, carbon dioxide and sulphur. Below ground, these are dissolved in magma, but they can be released as the magma rises towards Earth's surface, creating a threatening cloud above a volcano.

ASH EVERYWHERE

Sometimes, during the eruption itself, ash made of rocks and minerals is mixed up with the gases to create a thick, grey smoke-like substance.

VERDICT

Fake

OCEAN CURRENTS ARE CAUSED BY THE WIND

Help! The current's got me!

FACT OR FAKE?

The water in Earth's oceans is always on the move. If you're taking a swim, you might feel the currents carrying you along the surface, but there are also powerful currents deep underwater. They can flow just a little way or across whole oceans. But what sets them in motion?

THE SCIENCE

In the open ocean, as the wind blows it drags the surface water along in the same direction. The Sun warms tropical waters more than polar waters, which causes more movement and mixing. Many other factors play a part too, including the shape of the coastline, the ups and downs of the sea floor, and even Earth's spin.

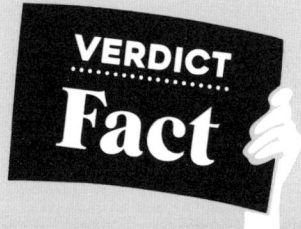

VERDICT

Fact

69

DAYS ON EARTH ARE GETTING LONGER

> Come back!

If you're in the half of the year that's heading towards summer, then of course it seems like the days are getting longer. In that case, however, it's really just that there are more hours of *daylight* in a day. But scientists believe that an actual day (24 hours) is increasing.

THE SCIENCE

The Moon is very gradually pulling away from our planet. As it does so, Earth slows down, increasing the length of time it takes to make one rotation on its axis – a day. It's happening very, very, *very* slowly – a day on Earth gets 1/75,000 of a second longer every year!

VERDICT
Fact

THE ICE AGE
WASN'T A ONE-OFF

> Really?
> I don't want
> to go through
> that again!

FACT OR FAKE?

We often refer to *the* Ice Age, and give it important-looking capital letters, as if it was the only one. But over Earth's 4.5 billion-year history there have been five ice ages that we know about.

THE SCIENCE

An ice age is a period in history where global temperatures were low enough to enable the ice caps to expand a lot. Earth was covered in glaciers and ice fields. An ice age could last for millions of years, but the last ice age (the one we tend to refer to with capitals!) only ended about 11,500 years ago.

MAN AND MAMMOTH

During the last ice age, humans drew pictures on cave walls showing woolly mammoths, woolly rhinos, woolly bears, and lots of other huge, warm, woolly creatures.

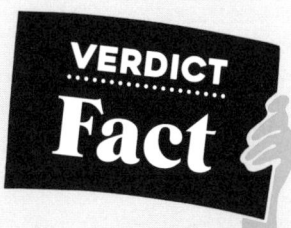

VERDICT
Fact

71

THERE'S SUCH A THING AS 'EARTHQUAKE WEATHER'

FACT OR FAKE?

Some people swear that you can tell when an earthquake is going to happen because of a phenomenon called 'earthquake weather' – hot, calm weather. In the past, people have also claimed that earthquakes happen after a period of strong winds and even meteors!

THE SCIENCE

Of course, there's no science at all to these claims. Statistics show that earthquakes happen in all sorts of weather conditions – hot, cold, rainy and dry. There's certainly no evidence of fiery meteor showers preceding earthquakes anywhere on Earth!

ANCIENT EARTHQUAKES

The idea has been around since the fourth century BCE, when ancient Greek philosopher Aristotle suggested that earthquakes were caused by wind trapped in underground caves.

VERDICT
....
Fake

EARTH'S MAGNETIC FIELD CAN ↑FLIP↓

FACT OR FAKE?

North is north and south is south – nothing can change that. Or can it …? In fact, throughout its history, Earth's magnetic poles have flipped every 200,000–300,000 years. The last time a big flip happened was 780,000 years ago. So, another one is long overdue.

THE SCIENCE

A 'geomagnetic reversal' sounds dramatic – possibly even fatal! But the truth is that you wouldn't really notice much difference. Apart from the fact that your compass needle would point north to Antarctica!

VERDICT
Fact

AROUND 85% OF SPECIES HAVEN'T BEEN DISCOVERED YET

FACT OR FAKE?

From bacteria and fungi to plants, animals and people, our planet is packed with living things. We've identified around 1.2 million different species of all forms of life. But scientists reckon this is less than 15 per cent of the total, and that there may be as many as 8.7 million different species on Earth.

THE SCIENCE

The reason so many species have yet to be seen is because there's a surprising amount of the planet that we haven't explored. What mysterious creatures might lurk in the unexplored ocean depths? What undiscovered insects nest in remote rainforest trees? And what about microscopic life forms that have escaped us just because they're too tiny to see?

DISCOVERY RATES

Hundreds of new species are discovered every year, but even at that rate, it's going to take a very long time to find them all ...

VERDICT

Fact

Imagine that you could drill a hole from where you're standing now, right through Earth's core to the other side of the world. If you jumped into the hole, how long would it be before you popped out the other side? About half a day?

IF YOU WENT STRAIGHT THROUGH THE MIDDLE OF EARTH, IT WOULD TAKE 12 HOURS TO REACH THE OTHER SIDE

THE SCIENCE

Despite the long distance – 12,742 km – it's a much quicker journey than that. Taking into account the increasing pull of gravity as you got closer to the centre of Earth, the whole ride would take just over 38 minutes.

GRAVITY FLIP

Gravity pulls you towards the centre of Earth, so really you'd never make it past that point, as you'd be pulled back the way you came!

VERDICT
....
Fake

76

NEARLY 30% OF EARTH
IS SILICON

There are 118 known chemical elements, and 92 of them can be found in fairly large quantities on Earth. But amazingly, just four elements make up 90 per cent of Earth's crust. Oxygen is the most common, but you might be more surprised to learn that silicon comes second, at 27.7 per cent.

THE SCIENCE

Silicon is an odd element. It's not a metal, but it's not a non-metal either! It's what scientists call a metalloid. Silicon has a solid, crystal-like structure in its natural form. One of the most common places you'll find it is on the beach, where it mixes with oxygen to form silica – the main ingredient in sand!

VERDICT
Fact

TIME ZONES MATCH EARTH'S LINES OF LATITUDE

FACT OR FAKE?

Lines of latitude measure distances north or south of the equator. Lines of longitude are used to measure how far east or west of a point something is, and it's these imaginary lines that are connected to time, not latitude.

THE SCIENCE

There are 360° of longitude (a full circle round Earth). Each geographical time zone covers 15° of longitude (24 hours). The time is slightly earlier or slightly later between neighbouring time zones. That's why it's midnight on one side of the planet and midday at the same time on the other side.

MEAN TIME

To keep things simple, many nations don't strictly stick to geographical time zones if a country covers several of them. For example, China crosses five geographical time zones, but runs to just one – Beijing Standard Time.

VERDICT
....
Fake

EARTH IS THE ONLY KNOWN PLANET THAT SUPPORTS LIFE

FACT OR FAKE?

The universe is big beyond imagining and it's possible that somewhere out there, other life forms exist. But the only thing we know for sure is that Earth is the only planet so far discovered that is capable of supporting life. And lots of things had to happen in just the right way at just the right time for that to be the case.

THE SCIENCE

The planet had to be just the right distance from its star, the Sun – not too hot and not too cold. The right mixture of gases had to form in the atmosphere so that living things could breathe. Other chemical ingredients also mixed to create life-supporting substances such as water.

Hi there!

VERDICT
Fact

THE CONTINENTS ARE MOVING

THE SCIENCE

The continents lie on Earth's huge tectonic plates (see page 50), which are constantly interacting. In some places, molten rock hardens into new sea floor in the cracks between the plates, making them wider. This is known as 'seafloor spreading'. As new rock widens the plates, the continents that lie on them are pushed further apart.

FACT OR FAKE?

It doesn't seem like the piece of earth you're standing on is slowly floating around, does it? But in fact all the continents are moving, in a process known as 'continental drift'.

VERDICT

Fact

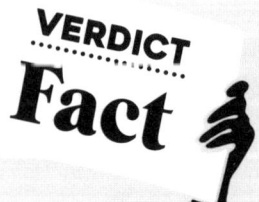

DRIFTING APART

North America and Europe are moving away from each other at a rate of about 2.5 cm a year – about the same speed that your nails are growing!

STALAGMITES GROW DOWN

AND

STALACTITES GROW UP

It's easy to get stalagmites and stalactites confused – after all, they sound pretty similar. But they're two different formations that grow in different directions. Remember – stalaCtites hang from the Ceiling and stalaGmites grow from the Ground.

THE SCIENCE

Stalactites look a bit like long icicles, with pointy ends. They form from the minerals in water as it slowly and continuously drips through the roof of a cave. Stalagmites are also mineral formations, but they build from the ground up, from deposits in the water that drips on to the cave floor. They have flatter or rounder tips.

VERDICT

Fake

THE ANDES IS THE LONGEST
MOUNTAIN RANGE

FACT OR FAKE?

The problem with records of Earth's extremes – highest, longest, biggest – is that people only look on the planet's surface. Really, the most extreme and impressive examples of just about everything are found in the underwater world.

THE SCIENCE

The longest mountain range is no exception. The Andes range stretches 7,000 km, but the Mid-Atlantic Ridge – a chain of underwater volcanoes in the Atlantic Ocean – more than doubles that, at 16,000 km.

VERDICT
Fake

BREAKING THE SURFACE

Some of the mountains in the ridge are so high that they sit above the surface, creating groups of islands.

EARTH IS RADIOACTIVE

Nuclear reactions are what power the Sun, and the rays it produces are what warm and light up Earth. Fortunately, the atmosphere filters out the most harmful radiation and we can live with what gets through. But our own planet also gives off its own heat through radioactive decay.

THE SCIENCE

Radioactive chemical elements can also be found in Earth's crust, including millions of tonnes of uranium, thorium and potassium. Certain types of these elements decay. As they do so, they create heat. This is what powers many of Earth's processes, including seafloor spreading (see page 80).

VERDICT

Fact

EARTH SPINS CLOCKWISE

FACT OR FAKE?

If you could hover over the North Pole, looking down on Earth, you'd see that our planet rotates *anticlockwise*, from west to east. The fancy scientific name for this is 'prograde rotation'.

THE SCIENCE

In this way, Earth is just like almost every other body in the backward-moving solar system. The Sun and most of the planets spin anticlockwise on their axes. The planets also move on an anticlockwise path around the Sun and the Moon moves anticlockwise around Earth.

BACKWARDS PLANET

Venus is the odd planet out – it rotates clockwise on its axis in a retrograde motion.

VERDICT
....
Fake

WE'VE FIXED THE HOLE IN THE OZONE LAYER

In 1985, scientists announced a dangerous discovery – there was HUGE hole in the ozone layer. This important part of Earth's atmosphere stops most of the Sun's harmful radiation reaching us (see page 83).

THE SCIENCE

The hole had been caused by people using chemicals known as chlorofluorocarbons (CFCs) in aerosol sprays. These were immediately banned and very slowly the hole began to heal. But it hasn't gone away. In fact, it continues to grow and shrink each year. In September 2020 it was measured at nearly 25 million square km. That's three times the size of the USA!

VERDICT
Fake

THE PACIFIC OCEAN IS BIGGER THAN ALL THE LAND ON EARTH

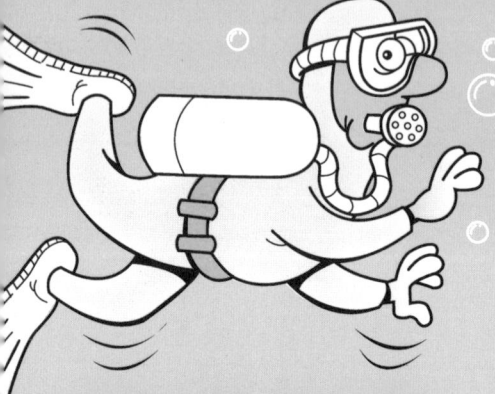

FACT OR FAKE?

It's hard to imagine that one single body of water could be bigger than all the solid ground on Earth put together. But the Pacific Ocean really is that big. Every continent could fit into the Pacific basin – with room to spare!

THE SCIENCE

The Pacific stretches more than 165 million square kilometres. If you put all the land on Earth together in one giant piece it would cover about 148 million square kilometres. The Pacific is also the deepest ocean, with an average depth of 4 km.

VERDICT
Fact

ROCK RECORDS
The Pacific is also the oldest ocean on Earth. Rocks have been found on the Pacific floor that are 200 million years old.

ONLY A QUARTER OF THE WATER ON EARTH IS FRESHWATER

With so much of Earth's surface covered in oceans, you'd expect there to be a lot more saltwater than freshwater. But the difference between the two is much greater than you might think. In fact, only 3 per cent of water on our planet is freshwater.

THE SCIENCE

Despite the many rivers and lakes all over Earth, most of its free-flowing freshwater is underground, just beneath the surface. More amazingly, 68 per cent of Earth's freshwater is locked up tight in the form of glaciers and ice caps.

VERDICT
Fake

87

IT CAN BE SUNNY AT MIDNIGHT

FACT OR FAKE?

It sounds like something out of science fiction, but the 'midnight sun' really exists. It's not something you'll spot just by staying up late and looking out of your bedroom window though – not unless you live in the Arctic or Antarctic Circle!

THE SCIENCE

Because of the tilt of the Earth, in scientific terms day and night at the North and South Poles are each six months long! There and in areas close to the poles, there are days in summer when the Sun is visible in the sky for nearly 24 hours at a time. The downside is that for six months of the year, it's always dark!

VERDICT
Fact

THE GLOBAL POPULATION GROWS BY MILLIONS EVERY YEAR

FACT OR FAKE?

It's a huge number, but it's true – around 140 million babies are born every year. That's 266 every minute, or more than four each second. Experts reckon that at these rates, the population will hit 11 billion by the year 2100.

THE SCIENCE

To properly measure population growth, you have to take away the number of people who have died from the number born. People are living longer than ever before. Good news for us! But with death rates lower than birth rates, overpopulation could eventually be a big problem for our planet.

RISING NUMBERS

When I started writing this sentence the global population was 7,873,885,819. By the time I got to the full stop, it was 7,873,885,944.

VERDICT

Fact

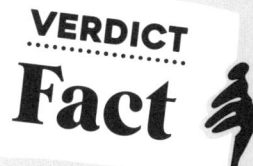

AT THE SOUTH POLE, EVERY DIRECTION IS NORTH

N

If you were standing right at the South Pole, you'd still be able to look up and down, look left and right and all around. It wouldn't seem any different from standing anywhere else on Earth (apart from how freezing cold you'd be). So how it is possible that every direction you looked in would be north?!

THE SCIENCE

Everything's relative. At the southernmost point on the planet, there's nowhere further south to go, so it makes sense that the only option is to go north. But this is only true *exactly* at the South Pole. Take a single step north (in any direction!) and you'd be back with all four points to choose from. East would be to your right and west to your left.

N

NORTH AND SOUTH
The opposite is true at the North Pole. There, the only direction you can choose from is south.

VERDICT

Fact

GLOSSARY

altitude – the height above a certain level, such as ground level or sea level

arc – a semicircle or horseshoe shape

atmosphere – the layer of gases that surround a very large object, such as a planet or a star

atom – the smallest particle of a chemical element; atoms are the building blocks of all matter

axis – an imaginary line through a planet, star or similar, around which it spins

basin – a dip in the earth that a body of water lies in

cataract – a large waterfall that drops straight down from the edge of a precipice

chemical element – a substance that contains just one type of atom, such as oxygen or iron

continent – one of Earth's seven large landmasses

core – the centre of a planet, star, moon or similar object

deflect – to make something change course or direction

deforestation – the cutting down of large areas of forest to make way for human activity

density – a measure of something's mass in relation to its volume (how much space it takes up)

DNA – a chemical found in living things that contains genetic information

dormant – describing a volcano that has not erupted for a very long time, but which could still erupt in the future

drought – a long period with little or no rainfall in a particular area

ecosystem – a community of living things and their environment

equator – an imaginary line around the middle of Earth, separating it into the northern and southern hemispheres

glacier – a large body of ice moving slowly down a slope or over a wide area of land

gravity – the force of attraction between two objects; its strength depending on the mass of the objects

heatwave – a long period of extremely hot weather

hemisphere – one-half of a ball-shaped or spherical object, such as Earth

ice cap – a thick layer of snow and ice that permanently covers an area

leap year – a year that occurs once every four years, which has 366 days, with 29 February as the extra day

magma – liquid rock that exists deep below the surface of Earth

mantle – the region of Earth between the crust and the core believed to consist of dense, semi-molten rocks

microbes – tiny living organisms such as bacteria or viruses, too small to be seen by the naked eye

mineral – a solid substance that occurs in nature

molten – describing things, such as metals, that have been heated to such a high temperature they become liquid

northern hemisphere – all of Earth that lies north of the equator

organism – any individual living thing, including animals, plants and single-celled life forms

photosynthesis – the process by which plants convert carbon dioxide and sunlight into oxygen

precipitation – water that falls to Earth in different forms (e.g. rain, snow, sleet, hail)

GLOSSARY (CONT.)

radiation – energy that moves from one place to another, usually as waves or particles; light, heat and sound are all forms of radiation

retrograde – describing something that moves backwards or opposite to the usual way

rotation – the movement of a planet round its axis (its spin)

sediment – small particles of rocks, minerals and other substances that are moved from one place to another by natural processes

sonar – a technology that can detect things underwater by sending out sound waves that are reflected back off objects

southern hemisphere – all of Earth that lies south of the equator

species – a group of living things that share similar characteristics and can breed with each other

sphere – ball shape

strait – a stretch of water that joins two larger bodies of water

tectonic plates – the huge pieces that Earth's lithosphere is broken up into, on which the world's oceans and continents sit

tropical – describing the parts of Earth that surround the equator

water vapour – water in the form of a gas

wavelength – the distance between the peak (or crest) of one wave and the next, for example, in light or sound waves

Hi there!

FURTHER INFORMATION

BOOKS

Planet Earth (Infomojis) by Jon Richards and Ed Simkins
(Wayland, 2021)

Planet Earth (Curious Nature) by Nancy Dickmann
(Franklin Watts, 2017)

Our Planet (Infographic: How It Works) by Jon Richards
(Wayland, 2016)

WEBSITES

www.bbcearth.com/bbc-earth-kids
The BBC Earth Kids website has loads of information about our
planet and everything that lives on it.

https://spaceplace.nasa.gov/menu/earth
Explore all sorts of information about Earth at NASA's Space
Place, with links to facts, games and videos.

**www.natgeokids.com/uk/discover/science/space/facts-
about-the-earth**
Find out more amazing facts about planet Earth on the National
Geographic Kids website.

www.worldometers.info/world-population
Go to the Worldometers website to see the global population
ticking up before your very eyes. Search the site for other
amazing real-time statistics about life on planet Earth.

INDEX